I0414694

Book Writing Ideas

How to Write and Publish a Book

Smit Chacha

ACKNOWLEDGMENTS

This book is a comprehensive guide in how to write and publish a book. I will guide you thoroughly in how to write a blogpost and convert it into a published book. You will learn all the best practices in how to become a successful author. I have written many books in my career as an author and   I want you to do the same.
Become a successful author with many book titles in your name.
Let's start writing…

What to Write About?

If you already know what to write then by all means start writing! Write all what you have in your mind, writing is fun when you know what you are writing about.

Once you have an idea of what to write it process is very easy and entertaining. Write everything that is in your mind, write the way you want to tell your story or whatever it is.

Write like you are talking to someone, you can also use some speech to text software if you are feeling lazy. But I would recommend that you start typing.

Typing is a lot of fun when you know what you are typing about. Writing a book makes the process so simple when you are in control of your writing.

You can start from the beginning, middle or by the last

page of your piece of art. Write in articles, each topic in one page. Then rearrange everything in one book.

This way you have the whole day of the month or year to write. Writing gets fun when you start typing. If you have a topic in your head put into writing.

Having things to write about in your head and putting into writing makes the process so easy that you will be so impress by yourself how much things have you wrote in just one minute.

Pages and pages of your book are being typed and you thought that your book will be so thin. Finding topics of your nice is easy when you know what you are typing.

Knowing the niche from top to bottom or having interest on that niche, in other words be a professional on that niche makes you the pro writer of the topic. And hence you can present it in a book.

You become a professional in that topic and people will start asking questions to you. In later chapters we will talk about how to use Social Media and blogs to engage with people and market your book.

Finding a Niche

To publish a book, you need a specific topic to write about, this is called a niche. Choose a niche and bullet point the sub topics or chapter of your book. Choosing a niche is the first step to write a book.

There are many categories that you can choose and you will need to know which category your niche seats into. When you are publishing your book, you need to specify in which category your book seats into.

You can choose from a non-fiction to fiction and its sub categories. Here are some examples of sub categories in the non-fiction area: health, diet, business, sports, etc.

To choose a niche you can use the internet to find ideas, however I would recommend that you write about stuff that you already know or are a fan about. Write about stuff that you are an expert, a follower or simply a fan about the topic.

It gets a lot easier to write stuff about that you already know. You can still research topics over the internet to fine tune your book publishing process.

A niche is the first thing that should come into your mind when writing a book. You can use a notepad to point out which things or chapters you will write about. A book can have many chapters and you as the author has to decide how you will organize the book.

The book is simple a pile of paper that has all the topics and things about the stuff you want to share to others. It is a kind of library where people can read and get all the information in one place.

You just have to write it and organize it. Writing a book takes time and you can write 1 chapter, or 1 article or just 1 page in your leisure time. After writing all the chapters all you need to do is organize it in 1 Microsoft Word file with a table of contents and publish it.

Finding the Right Category of your Book

Before starting writing your book you should decide in which category it will fit in. There are many categories to choose from, from non-fiction to fiction.

Take some time to decide which category your book will be. Choosing a perfect niche category of your book takes time. Sometimes you might find in a situation where there are multiple categories that your book fits in. Take some time and carefully choose the niche of your book.

A good way to do this is to temporarily fit a niche or title of your book and when the whole book is finished choose the right category. It is not an easy process it takes time and it should be done carefully.

Finding the Right Category of your Book

While spending time writing your book you will eventually find the right category that your book will fit in. Just keep writing with a premature titled in mind.

The title or subtitles of your book can change from time to time. After finishing your book, you may find in s situation where you notice that you have found a better title or subheading of your book.

With experience you will find this process a lot easier and automatic. Just keep writing the book and you can start from the beginning, middle or at the very end of your book.

With time you will find the writing and publishing process a lot quicker and fun. The first book always is a lot more tough and tedious.

Just keep writing and with time you will find writing to be fun and with time you will publish a lot of books this way.

From Blogpost to a Published Book

There are many ways to publish a book, you can start from a simple notepad or from a blog. I recommend starting from a blog and convert your blogposts into a published book (paperback and digital). This way of publishing a book will give you a slight advantage in terms of marketing.

Marketing a book while still in working order is a good way to create a buzz about your book. Creating a blog these days is very easy and affordable. You can start from a simple WordPress blogpost and later on convert your posts into a book.

There are many other blog platforms, WordPress is the most commonly used and it is easy to install and use. You can post your blogposts daily, weekly or monthly bases it is all up to you. The great thing about posting a blogpost is that people will start following your blog and you will get engagements and popularity. Once your blog starts getting traffic, marketing your book will be a lot simpler.

You will also create a Facebook Fan Page and a Twitter Page where you will directly be in contact with your fans and readers.

Marketing your books while still typing will not only create excitement but also useful comments which you can incorporate in your next book chapters. Since the launched of social media platforms marketing your books became a lot easier. Use this useful resource for your useful advantage. If you are blogging a blogpost do not forget to market it on other social media platforms.

Internet, webpages, blogs, search engines and other media platforms work entirely with links. Which means you will also need to market your WordPress blog and this can be done with SEO.

This was an introduction of how you can market your book while still working on the project. Later we will discuss all the above topics in greater detail.

How to Start Writing your Book

There are loads of ways to start writing a book, there is no right or wrong. All authors work differently, however there are some tips that I can share with you that will speed up the process or give you an idea in how to start engaging with your book.

Normally I start by brainstorming ideas or topics about what I am going to write about. Many authors find this method easy to organize.

You can start by typing your keywords or topics in a notepad (paper or computer). I normally open a notepad on my computer and set the topics. This document will change over time, as I start writing new ideas or sub topics while publishing my book.

Having a starting point with some notes or topics in hand makes it easy to start writing a book. Internet is a good way to get topic or sub topic ideas of what you are going to write about.

A simple search on Google will give you a ton of keywords of the niche that people are searching for. You can also start a blog and write your articles, excerpts or even the whole book to engage with your audience.

A blog makes it easy to save your work while access it anywhere in the world, all you need is internet. You can also at the end of writing everything on your blog convert it to a membership website, where users can find your writing online while being a member or a fan of your book. This way at the end of typing your work you will have a paperback version of you book, a digital version and a membership website.

To market your book, you can use social media websites, such as Facebook an easy way to engage with your audience. You can also subscribe your readers and add them to your email mailing list so they can get updates of your new upcoming books.

Note: Writing a book or a blog takes time, and people fail because they rush things. Write on your spare time and do one task at a time. Do not start creating a blog, Facebook page, etc. in one day!

How to Write a Book (Page Formatting)

There are many ways to write a book, you can start with pen and paper, a typewriter or straight to a computer. I normally write on a computer with certain page formatting settings. These settings speed up my process of publishing the book.

I do not write in any typical order, sometimes I start from the middle or at the end of the book. At the time of publishing I just organize those files in to an order that I want the reader to read.

For example, if my book has 100 pages, I would have at least 100 different documents under 100 different titles that are not any sort of order. At the end I would just organize those 100 titles in a single Word document.

Publishers will have a wide range templates of each

various book sizes that you can choose from. My books are typically an A5 size, where each page has around 250 words.

I write my books on a Word document that is A4 with 0.5 margins top, bottom, left and right. It means that I have the whole document to type. Each page would have an average of 800 to 1000 words. This means by the end of the day I would have written between 4 to 5 pages of my book.

This means a typical 100 pages book would have around 25000 words, or 25 A4 pages (from the settings that I mentioned above).

When it comes to organize the book into the publishers template the formatting will be done automatically. This means all you have to transfer your unsorted work into 1 publishers template document. We will cover this in a greater detail in later chapters.

Writing a book takes time and as I said earlier you do not need to type from the beginning. You can start at any given page of your book; all you have to do is organize at the end when everything has been written.

My preferred method is to write blogposts and convert it into a book or a membership website. This way I can create a buzz about my findings. Social media and blogs are the easiest way to create a buzz about your book and this can be done while your work is still in progress.

Adding Pictures to your Book (Image Quality)

An image speaks a thousand words and it is always nice to have some pictures inside your book. Adding graphics is very easy, you can use Microsoft Word to embed images to your document.

Picture quality matters when publishing a book (either is digital or paperback). Ideally your graphics should be at least 300dpi picture quality.

Anything that looks good on your computer screen when printing the quality fades out, especially on those low-quality pictures. You can easily create graphics in Adobe Photoshop and change the picture quality or dpi for print design. DPI stand for dot per inch.

There are also free online tools that you can use to increase or decrease image dpi. All you have to do is upload your graphic and change the parameters to 300 dpi and download the image. Just search image dpi converter on Google. You will find hundreds search results.

I create my own graphics for my books, graphics that will be inside my book and the book cover. Some prefer to hire a graphic designer. If that is your case you can ask your graphic designer to create images in better print quality or 300 dpi.

I find Adobe Photoshop to be the best tool to create book covers and other graphics. You can also buy digital graphics and images online and for free (royalty free images). Just search buy pictures online or do a search on Google images with the keywords that you are looking for. You can use those pictures on your book cover and inside pages.

Remember picture quality or dpi will vary from publisher to publisher. As they have different types of printers. But generally speaking, 300dpi is a good quality picture for print. Read your publisher guidelines for image quality requirements and follow your publisher rules.

Lastly, I just want to stress out that many publishers offer in house graphic design department which you can use for a minimal cost or even for free. Just ask your publisher for this if you are having difficulty in designing your book cover and inside pages imagery.

Engaging on Social Media while Writing your Book

Not every author uses this method while the work is under production, however I find this method to be very rewarding. Many authors prefer market their book once the book is published.

There is nothing wrong in that method, it is less time consuming. I prefer to market my books while the writing is still going on. I find this method a lot easier afterwards and a lot more rewarding.

I can get a lot of ideas and comments from my readers and embed their thoughts on my ongoing process of publishing the book.

Engaging with your audience on social media is a lot simpler when you have a Facebook Fan Page of the book that you are still writing about. Create a blogpost of each articles of your book and upload a link to social media and start engaging with your fans.

You can also tweet on Twitter; however, I use Facebook more often than Twitter. The concept is simple to get a small group of fans before getting the book published.

You can do this task once a week, once every two weeks or once a month, etc. you choose. But do not overdo it, do not get your whole book on social media, just a few lines or excerpts that will be on your book.

At the end of blog posting you can turn your blog into to a fans members area where they can purchase a membership and get even further content from you. It is up to you to choose this method of marketing while still writing your masterpiece.

You can choose to write your book and then do all the marketing after the book is available on the market. As I said before not every author prefers my method of publishing. And you as an author have every right in how you want to market your books.

While Writing a Book (Style of Writing)

As I said earlier, writing a book takes time and you can start from any given point (beginning, middle or the very end of your book pages).

The writing style varies from author to author, some like to write in 3rd person while other in first. Some prefer to write is a shape of articles and rearranged them and form a table of contents. While other write is a shape of a story telling style.

My books are mostly article based. I write articles and rearranged them afterwards while forming a table of contents. This is my preferred method of writing a book.

The advantage of this writing style is that you can easily start from any giving point in time in time of your book. I can start an article and rearranged it and positioned in the middle or at the very end of the book.

This is how I mostly write my books. **Note:** This book was also written that way.

It is all up to you how to choose the writing style of you book, you can choose to write in a form of a story telling, the biggest disadvantage that I found is that writing style is that it is a little trickier to start writing a story telling book from the middle or later pages.

I found writing is an article shaped book a lot easier to write, but it is all up to you.

My article shaped writing style means that each article title of my book will be the chapters of my finished table of contents. This means a chapter could be just 1 or more pages.

Microsoft Word has a really good tool to create table of contents, all you need to do is rearranged your work into

1 Word document and click on table of contents tool and the software will do its magic. Your whole project will automatically be presented with this amazing tool. I will cover this software tool in a greater detail in later chapters.

Turning Your Work in to a Subscription

We have talked about marketing your book while still in progress, how you can create a WordPress blog and publish your work online to create a buzz. We also touched on social media, how it can create an audience for your book.

Now I want to highlight how you can transform your WordPress blog into a subscription. Subscription simply means that in order for your readers to read your work they must register on your blog. You will have their personal details such as name and email address.

On the registration page you can auto subscribe your readers into your mailing list. We will touch on email marketing in later chapters. But for now, I just want you to know that you can auto subscribe your members to an email list.

There are many content management systems out

there, if you choose WordPress (which is my preferred CMS). You will find plenty of free and premium plugins to create a subscription-based blog. Just search and install the plugin.

You can choose how your membership-based blog will work, for instance you can select certain amount of free and premium content. Later you can also create a mobile app for your membership website, we will touch on mobile marketing in later chapters.

And when your book is finished you can find a publisher and publish your book online, we will also cover how to find a publisher and how to publish your book in later chapters.

Finding a Publisher or Self Publish your Book

The hard work is done you can complete your book, now it is time to publish your book. There are couple of options: find a publisher or self-publish your book.

Sending your work to a publisher means you will earn royalties and the publisher gets his cut. Self-publishing your book means you will have the full royalties.

There are advantages of having a publisher, for instance you just have to send your work and they will distribute to all channels, including digital and paperback. Some publishers also offer marketing services.

One of my favorite publishers is LULU. You can upload you work online and set the price and the publisher will do the rest. You will accumulate royalties and you will be paid by PayPal or cheque at the end of the month.

The publisher will distribute your work in multiple channels (online retailers, distributers and libraries). Including Amazon, Google, Barnes and Noble, Kobo and many others.

You will get a free ISBN when you publish your work through LULU.

If self-publishing is in your mind then Amazon KDP is the best choice. You will be able to distribute your paperback work in Amazon multiple channels alongside a kindle version. The advantage of self-publishing via Amazon KDP is that you will have a variety of options to market your book.

Another advantage of Amazon KDP is that you can enroll your work to Amazon Select and earn royalties based on pages viewed by an Amazon Unlimited subscriber. Each month Amazon will declare the global fund allocated to

Amazon Select.

If you chose to publish via LULU, currently you have no option to select Amazon Select royalties. Which is a big disadvantage!

Note: once you enroll your kindle book to Amazon Select you cannot publish any digital version of the book in any other retailer. It must be an Amazon Exclusive.

Publishing your Book

When it comes to publishing your book certain page formats must be considered. It does not matter if you are publishing via a publisher or self-publishing your books.

LULU and other publishers will have a template which you can download and publish your book. Amazon KDP also offers similar content.

Publishing a digital version of your book can vary, some provide a free software which you can convert your word document file into a digital version.

Amazon KDP offers kindle create software where you can convert your word document into a kindle book. If publishing via LULU, they offer free conversation tools when uploading your work to them.

They will distribute your both paperback and digital versions to their channels. For Amazon KDP you need to upload your paperback book in word or pdf format and then use the free Kindle Create software to convert for word document into a kindle edition.

The process usually takes few minutes and within 72 hours your book is live on Amazon and their channels. Publishing via LULU can take up to 60 days to get your book in all their distribution channels.

Enrolling your book in Kindle Select can also take up to 72 hours but usually you will find that your book will be live within few hours.

You can choose to create your own covers or select templates; I prefer to create my own covers and it should be at least 1200 x 1600 pixels and 300 dpi.

Marketing your Books

Amazon KDP offers you to create offers for your book, for instance you can offer your book for free or for a sale price for a period of time. You can also offer a free digital version of your book when someone purchases a paperback version.

There is so much you can do to market your books. Engage on social media, newsagents, radio, etc.

Over time you will accumulate royalties from your various published titles.

This is the best time to become a successful author! Get on board!

ABOUT THE AUTHOR

Smit Chacha has written multiple books in his career as an author. He started as a successful blogger and later he become an author with many book titles in his name.

www.ingramcontent.com/pod-product-compliance
Lightning Source LLC
Chambersburg PA
CBHW020333290526
45785CB00007B/3046